Love &
Blessings

[signature]

MW01231380

Walk
in
Peace

Transforming My Life's Experiences

Tami Principe

Great Books, Defined.

WinePress Publishing (PO Box 428, Enumclaw, WA 98022) functions only as book publisher. As such, the ultimate design, content, editorial accuracy, and views expressed or implied in this work are those of the author.

Unless otherwise noted, all Scriptures are taken from the *Holy Bible, New International Version*®, *NIV*®. Copyright © 1973, 1978, 1984 by Biblica, Inc.™ Used by permission of Zondervan. All rights reserved worldwide. www.zondervan.com

Scripture references marked KJV are taken from the *King James Version* of the Bible.

Scripture references marked NASB are taken from the *New American Standard Bible*, © 1960, 1963, 1968, 1971, 1972, 1973, 1975, 1977 by The Lockman Foundation. Used by permission.

ISBN 13: 978-1-4141-1970-0
ISBN 10: 1-4141-1970-4
Library of Congress Catalog Card Number: 2010939671

I dedicate this book to both my sons. I hope that now they will better understand the events that happened, because they are grown men. Regardless how hard our life was, I am proud of you. I enjoyed our bonfires, football games and basketball games, our card games and swimming. You grew up way too fast. I love you both dearly. I also dedicate this book to my husband, for being so patient while I worked on it and my website and radio talk show.

Contents

Making Me

Chapter 1

Growing Up

THIS IS MY own personal story. In the following pages you will find courage, sympathy, empathy, and a growing yearning to understand the past, the present, and the future. I will not mention names. The point of this book is not to point fingers, but to learn and to teach—and to overcome all things that you thought were not possible.

To all the people who ever knocked someone else's dream because you were too afraid to dream yourself, I hope you find a heart. I want to give people the courage and the hope to pursue their dream and never listen to the negativity. The negativity is a tool that can only drown your desire. Listen to your heart and feel your dream. Never give up on yourself.

I grew up poor and didn't know my father. That brought all kinds of abandonment issues that lasted pretty much all my life. When I really reflect and think back, I can see all the times it affected me. Even when I thought it didn't. If I am in a crowded place, that is my biggest fear—to be left alone, to be abandoned, to know absolutely no one. To be scared and left feeling helpless, just like that little child. That was the same feeling I experienced as a little girl—that same sense of abandonment.

I was always the independent type. I really didn't have any friends until I got older. That was how it always was. As a child of five, I remember putting people's groceries in their car for a tip at the local A & P that was real close to my house. At the end of the day, I would buy those white powder donuts as a treat for myself. They were a dime back then.

At school I was always in trouble. I remember the principal always walking the halls. I used to squeeze into a locker so he wouldn't see me. If you were caught in the hall, you were in trouble. That was back when they used wooden boards to hold open the door to the fire escape. That brought some fresh air into a stuffy room. And if you were caught talking, or anything else, the teacher would spank you with that board. I'm glad they don't do that anymore.

My favorite place to go was to church. I couldn't wait for the church doors to open. It was the safest place in my world that I could go. I used to sit in the pews and listen to every word that came out of that preacher's mouth. He told stories, and they sang songs. I didn't go into the kids' classrooms. I wanted to sit with the grownups, so I did. Sometimes the preacher would yell some of his stories, but that just meant he was really trying to get people to understand what he was talking about. My brother left crying, because he didn't understand. He thought the preacher was yelling at him. But I always came back every chance I could. I wanted to hear another one of his stories. Even now as an adult, I still love for my husband to tell me a story—but no one ever tells one like that preacher man did.

I grew up in Harvey, and we were pretty poor. For a long time I remember we ate hot dogs and pork 'n' beans for every meal—every breakfast, lunch, and dinner. I used my mom's old curler box to eat on. But we never went hungry. Back then, when you were on food stamps, they gave you food stamp coins too. And at the A & P, they had S & H Green Stamps that you got when you bought something. People used to save them and buy things with them.

I remember walking home from school one day when I was in first grade. At that time they had an actual police officer as a crossing guard. I asked the officer, "What happens to a man's things once he dies?"

"They would go to a relative," the officer said. I responded, "What if he didn't have any relatives?" The officer said that it would go to the city.

"He works his whole life to get whatever he has, and it ends up that the city just takes it," I said. "That's not fair!"

He must have noticed the expression on my face when I said that. I must have really surprised the officer, because he started questioning me. "Do you know someone who's hurt?"

"No," I said. "I was just wondering what happens to their stuff." "Well then," he said, "you just move along and don't worry about that." I learned at a tender age that possessions are just that—possessions. Once you die, it really doesn't matter what you have. It's just possessions.

I used to lie awake at night and think about the other kids who were in foster homes. I always wondered what their life was like. When I got out of school I would go babysit and after that, it was time to get home and go to bed. I hated my life as a child; I always wanted to be in a foster home. I would pray every night, "Dear Lord, please don't make me wake up. Or if I wake up, please let me wake up in a foster home." It never happened. I always woke up in the same bed in the same place—home.

I began acting out more at school; my grades fell from good ones to very poor. I wouldn't talk to anyone. I started running away when I was young. My friends were always the best. They never asked any questions, and they brought me food. At night I slept in the backseat of cars—or a friend would sneak me into their house when their parents fell asleep. The ending was always the same—I had to go back home. They would find me. Each time they asked, "Did you learn anything?" My response was always, "Yeah, I should have brought more candy bars."

That was a long time ago, but I still remember it like it was yesterday. That's when I learned about compassion and empathy. When you are lying there cold and hungry and afraid—even then you think about people who have it harder than you. I think that's what the preacher told me about in one of his stories. Always be grateful for what you have! Some people don't have anything. I at least had shelter for the night.

One time something came up missing. We were all asked who took it; but no one fessed up so we all got the belt. It still hurts thinking about it. That's when I learned about owning up to something. I didn't take it and I never would, and I don't care how much I was beat. Later, the thing was found; it had just been misplaced. But I knew that inside me, no matter what ever happened in the future, I would always take responsibility for my actions. I would own up to them because I would never want anyone else to suffer because of something I did.

Chapter 2

My Guiding Strength

W E ALL HAVE one special person in the family who is our favorite. No one is really supposed to favor anyone else, but I did have my favorites. My Aunt Ruby and Aunt Beatrice (Bea for short) were my favorites, and both were strong women.

My Aunt Ruby was always in her kitchen breaking off green beans into a pan. I remember thinking, *She eats a lot of green beans; every time I see her she's breaking them off into a pan.* Aunt Ruby had diabetes—and developed complications from it. Once they started operating on the gangrene, they just kept going, and she never walked again. Even with her being in that wheelchair, Aunt Ruby always smiled at me. I thought of her house like it was my home. She had a porch swing on the front porch and a swing set in the backyard right by her garden. And when you were bad, she made you get the switch from the tree.

My Aunt Bea was such a special women. I can still hear her laugh. I miss her so dearly. She always called me "Young'n." I followed her around everywhere. It was from Aunt Bea that I learned that a woman can do anything. Aunt Bea was a great cook. She kept up a huge garden and taught me how to fish. My Aunt Bea was a great foster mom as well. Yes, my Aunt Bea could do it all.

I remember times when I was frustrated with something, Aunt Bea would say, "You just ain't learned how to do that yet," and laugh. "Young'n, you're a sight!" She had the patience of a saint. I truly feel that she loved me.

The rest of my early years were just about going to school, which I used more as a social scene, and working. I was working full-time hours, in addition to going to school. There was no time to play, and I was never allowed to.

After school each day, I had a set time I had to be home. It was timed. I remember walking home from school one day with some friends; I didn't want to take the bus home. It took longer to walk than to ride the bus, and that day I was behind schedule. I ran for six blocks straight to make sure I walked in the door on time.

Even so, I was two minutes late. That was not a good thing. Then it started "Where were you?" "How come you're late?" And then someone knocked on the door. It was one of my friends. I didn't expect it because they were all laughing and were making fun of me because I was running home.

"It's one of your friends. Tell them you can't go out."

"No, I'm not going to tell them," I said. "You tell them."

And so he told them. I figured I was already in trouble so what the heck. It really didn't matter. That is when I learned how to make good use of my time. Being late got me into trouble, so I would make sure that I was always on time for everything. I started looking at my choices, thinking, *I could be doing this or I could be doing that.* I just couldn't waste any time. So I didn't, ever.

I held so much anger inside. Finally, one day I saw him going to his car. I picked up a rock and threw it. I was so close. It cost me $250.00 to have the windshield fixed on that old Mustang. I was only in the 8th grade, but I learned that anger cost money.

I had a hard time staying in school. It felt like being in prison. I always needed a window so I could look out. At home I finally started tying the sheets together and throwing them out my bedroom window. I was getting better and better at it; each time tying them quicker than the previous time. One time when I was trying to make my escape, I got a phone call. They used to turn the electrical circuit breaker off and on for my bedroom. That's how I knew it was time to come downstairs for something. So I went downstairs to take my phone call and there it was, hanging in the window, my bed sheet. My heart sank. I'd never seen it from downstairs before. I would have to learn to be more careful.

I hurried through my phone call and removed all traces of the bed sheets, just in case. That is where I learned the art of never leaving a trace of anything. Just pick up after yourself, which I always did.

The years coming up were harder. I wasn't allowed to date, and there were some guys who wanted to date me. I had gotten better at tying the sheets together so I could get some free time. My mom babysat at night, so I would just go with her and come home when she did. That was my freedom. I felt like a prisoner free, finally free, if only for a little while. With this new-found freedom came only trouble. I was out drinking. Actually, I did a lot of drinking. I also smoked pot a little. And I wrote. I wrote a lot. I wrote poems and articles about wanting and wishing. I had showed my guidance counselor at school my writings. He was impressed, so the following week he called me to his office. He said that he had read all of my articles and poems and that he wanted to forward them to a publisher, so they could take a look. I said fine, but never expected anything to come of it. Two weeks later, the guidance counselor again called me into his office. There was a man there wearing a brown suit. He was from a publishing company. He did all the talking. He explained that he published writings for a booklet that alcohol and drug rehab places used. He said he wanted to publish my writings, so I signed a contract with him.

That was all I remember because that weekend I had met a boy, I got home late that night, and when I did, all my belongings were outside. I ended up moving in with my new boyfriend that night. There was no turning back now. For three years I never went back to that town. I didn't go back to the school to get any of my writings out of my locker, or anything.

Chapter 3

My New Life

I HAD MOVED in with my new boyfriend. I thought life was going to be great! It all started out great. No problems, no worries, just young love. But one night when I was working, I started fainting. I spoke to my mom a couple of days later and told her about what happened. "Oh, no," she said, "you better get to the doctor's." So I did. I was pregnant. I was only 17.

I didn't know a lot about what I should do when I was pregnant, so I was still very active. Then one day while I was playing Frisbee outside with everyone, I suddenly didn't feel good. I went and lay down. I was cramping, and it only got worse. I ended up losing that baby. It hurt like hell. I wish I would have known.

Things started getting worse. By that time my boyfriend had proposed not once, but a few times. I kept telling him no. It seemed back then there was a lot of partying and drinking going on. Either we were drinking at our friend's house or the party was where we were at. Pretty soon he started drinking more.

I got another job, in a factory. It was 90 degrees outside, which made it 106 inside the factory. Also, the air-conditioners from the office were blowing hot air on us, so I figured it was about 115 degrees inside that factory. I learned at that point that I was going to be working in an office. And I never worked in another factory again.

I became pregnant again. This time I was very cautious during my whole pregnancy. I fainted a lot, and I had a hard time gaining weight until toward the end. I had a 6-pound, 4-ounce baby boy.

He was a handful from the start. He had his nights and days mixed up, and he was colicky. For six months, I feel like I did nothing but walk the floor with him. We were poor, but we scraped up enough money to buy a trailer. It was small, but it was ours. Then my husband lost his job and things started getting real bad. About the same time he started drinking again.

That's when the abuse started. There was a lot of it. I was beat down. No hopes and no dreams. Life remained like that through one more miscarriage and the birth of another son. I had left many times in between, but I always came back. Fourteen years later, I finally walked away from that man. I never looked back. I got my divorce and took back my name.

Changes

Chapter 4

Starting Over

I KEPT THE house that we had been renting. I worked two jobs, raising my two sons the best I could. I put my sons in counseling because my oldest son showed signs of a bad anger problem. When I spoke with the counselor, I learned that it is typical of a child to react this way when the abuser is no longer in the home. The child is not living in fear anymore, but they don't know how to cope with the built-up anger, so they let it out—often on the people they love. My older son would end up having a lot of problems. He began drinking when he got older, and I have had to call the police on him numerous times. I was only 110 lbs and very frail, and he was six feet tall. He had tried to take control of my house more than once. He even broke out all my windows in my truck.

As a single mom, it was hard enough for me to put food on the table. It was also hard going from one job right to another. It was hard to take my pay and use it all to pay the babysitter and the bills—and worry about what my kids were doing. My child support was $100 every two weeks. My job paid me $7.00 an hour, and I paid the babysitter $2.00 an hour. That meant there were no baseball games, no school pictures, no extras of any kind. We didn't even use our knives; we didn't have any meat to cut.

My children knew I worked two jobs. They knew what time I left for work and what time I'd be home. I had surprised them periodically, so I always knew what they were up to. I would come home early from work and park my truck in the garage instead of leaving it in the driveway. They were always surprised when I did that. I could always tell how many kids were in the house by the amount of rocks that were swept up from the driveway. We played basketball and football and had our bonfires. We had a lot of good times and a lot of good memories were made. They never really had a lot, and they never asked for anything either, but we sure had some good times too.

Chapter 5

Family Trouble

MY OLDEST SON was regularly babysitting for my sister's children. But he started coming home later and later. I called and said that he had to be home at a decent time; he had school the next day. It kept happening, finally, I said that he was not going to be babysitting anymore.

That's when it happened. My brothers came over one night. They had brought a twelve-pack, and we were talking. They kept saying things like, "Kids do stupid things sometimes." But I could not understand what they were saying.

The next morning a DCFS worker showed up at my door. I invited her in. We sat down, and she brought up a list of allegations that had been made against me. I invited her to walk around and inspect my house, which was always spotless. I showed her

21

the refrigerator and cabinets. Then she noticed the empty twelve-pack container by the garbage. I told her that my brothers had been over last night and had brought it with them. My friends knew I never kept any alcohol in my house because my son would find it—and that's the last thing I needed with his temper.

My ex-husband had my youngest son for the weekend, and my oldest was still at my sister's house. The case worker proceeded to tell me that the child had to be out of the house for 24 hours while they investigated. She was referring to my oldest son only. I looked at the case worker and told her that she's not going to bring him back. She said she had to—it's the law—and left me her card. It turned out that she didn't bring him back. Upon the advice of people in the industry, I went to the police department and filed a missing persons report. I had not heard from him in days. But when I got home from work I was delivered papers—court papers. My sister had filed an emergency petition for my son to be permanently placed with her. My ex-husband was also brought up in the court documents.

This forced us to join together and go to court. The man I was trying to get away from was forced back into my life by the same person who said she was protecting my son, against what? He was already out of the house. It didn't make sense and it was devastating. Life sure is hard sometimes. And it even gets harder when you can't figure out why people do the things they do. You have to wonder. Is it for attention? Jealousy? Or is there some sort of mental disorder? Either way, you can only control *you*. You can only play with the cards that you were dealt with. So as with everything in life, you have to pull yourself back up by your bootstraps and carry on. I guess it's true what they say: "What doesn't kill you only makes you stronger." I know in the book of Matthew it says to forgive. I can see one day forgiving, but I know I will never forget.

Chapter 6

My Day in Court

WHEN OUR CASE was called, an attorney started saying all of the bad things about me. Like how I beat and starved my son. I said, "Your honor, I don't even know where my son is. He was supposed to be brought back and never was." I handed her my missing person's report. The first attorney stormed out of the courtroom, he was so mad.

The next attorney came up to bat. He started to take over from where the other one left off. He said all of those things that the other one had.

I just looked at him and said, "Why would I do all of those things to just one child? I have two children. I treat them both the same. I love them both the same." He also walked out of the courtroom, just as angry. He obviously thought I had only one child.

The last attorney was still there. But the look on his face was not the same as when he had entered that court room almost seven hours earlier. There was a lot of legal talk that I wasn't familiar with. The judge looked at me and said that we were all going into the conference room: me and my ex and my sister, and the guardian *ad litum* for my son.

The court advocate pulled me to the side and said, "I know you are deeply hurt by all of this, but I have to tell you that your sister will be walking in this room shortly." The advocate said I should not even look at my sister and shouldn't say anything. She said that she understood the anger I must be feeling. The advocate was right. It turns out that my oldest son wanted to still have contact with my sister. So visitation was set at that point. And I sent my oldest son to live with his father for a while.

I didn't trust anyone anymore. I have always wanted to be an attorney. That day, I had to represent myself. I could not afford to hire counsel, and I was so deeply embarrassed by all of it.

Needless to say, that was it for the family parties, like at Christmas and Thanksgiving, still to this day. Trust me, I'm okay with it. The one who feels left out the most is my youngest son. He didn't deserve any of this.

That all happened fifteen years ago. Since then I have had to call the police and change my phone numbers when my sister tried contacting me. I wish only to be left alone by her and her children. What was done to me was pure evil. And I have zero tolerance for anyone who messes with anybody's kids. That's the number one rule in life.

I did try, about two years later, to see everyone. My husband at the time thought it was a good idea. I agreed to try, but it didn't turn out. I didn't trust them, and I didn't feel comfortable. So that was that. I knew I wasn't going to try anymore. I will continue to wish only the best for them. I do believe in karma and I don't want any bad things coming back on me, ever. You can drive yourself crazy trying to figure out the thought process and the actions of others. So don't even try. Just go about what you do and don't pay no mind to others, especially if there's bad intent. However, I do think that praying for your enemies and forgiving them are the hardest of life's lessons, but they are the most beneficial in making yourself heal.

Chapter 7

Caring for Others

MY MOM DEVELOPED breast cancer. While I was taking her to her radiation appointments and doing things with and for her, all she would do is bring up my sister's name. What a stab that was. I had been there for my mom's surgeries, her radiation, her chemo, and changed her bandages—and she always brought up my sister's name. My sister was never around for any of these. Even my husband would question it: "Why does your mom bring up her name to you?" He said, "It's like she's rubbing it in your face."

He was right. So I completely walked away. I stopped helping her. I told my mom that if she needed any more help, she could call my sister. I must say, it's been nice not worrying about anyone else for a change. This was a first in my life. From this experience I learned that even a bum on the street will probably be less likely to hurt you than your own family. They expected me to forgive and forget. Would you? Although it has been years, I have been able to forgive, but sometimes the memories bring back the pain.

The next nine years I lived with my youngest son. My oldest would come and stay awhile, but then leave. I can honestly say that after the turn of events, I didn't trust him. Trust is never a given. It must be earned. There is always hope that with time it may be earned again.

When it comes to family, you always have greater expectations of them. You have no expectations of a stranger. That's what makes it so hard when dealing with family issues. You just expect to be treated differently and expect different things.

I don't know a lot about family, but I do know this. You should be able to count on them for something. Everyone has their own way of thinking, their own way of doing things. And there is nothing wrong with that. As long as it doesn't hurt anyone else. I think it would help if people kept an open mind and were receptive to other's wants and needs. I think there will always be differences, but it's how you deal with them that matters the most.

Chapter 8

My Empty House

I MOVED IN with my new husband. My old house was empty. When I had dropped my youngest off at his dad's house, I saw his income tax papers lying on the table. The previous year, he had made $60,000. But he was paying child support based on a $7.00 an hour job. It turns out that there was a form that when he left his old job, he was supposed to take it to his new job. But he never did. I took him back to court for more child support. Three months later, my youngest son said, "I want to go live with Dad."

I felt like I'd been hit with a ton of bricks. So I took a deep breath and composed myself. I didn't want my son to see how much he just hurt me. I said, "That's fine, go ahead. Let's get your things together and I will make arrangements with the school."

I knew why he was going, but I wasn't going to tell my son. He had to form his own opinions about his father on his own. If I told my son that he couldn't go, he would have just ended up hating me.

My oldest son went to live with my sister and help her raise all her kids. My youngest son now lived with his father. My house was now empty. I had a hard time with that. I had been the one going into their rooms and making sure the covers were pulled up tight so they wouldn't get cold. I had followed the bus while crying when it left to take them to camp. I cried so much when they were gone. It took me a long time to write them letters because I kept getting the paper wet.

My sons ended up coming to live with me and my new husband. They would stay awhile, work for awhile. Our rules were simple. You work, pay rent, and stay out of trouble. They both came and went a few times. Now they are older.

My oldest son still has issues. He is growing up, though. It took me almost a month to get him into rehab. He walked out just seven days later. After that he was arrested for a misdemeanor, and the following week he was arrested again.

I was not going to bail him out. He had to start thinking about the road he was on. He was twenty-eight years old.

I received a call from a family friend. She said, "Did you know that your son was arrested?"

I said, "Yes, he came to my house at three in the morning, and the police followed him there and arrested him in my house. "

She said, "Your family wants to know if you're going to get him out."

I said, "No, he's a grown man. He got himself in there; he can get himself out." It wasn't about the money. His fine was less than $100. It was the principle. He needed to figure out what he was doing with his life. He had to have time to think—and in jail is where he needed to be to figure it out.

Because it was just a misdemeanor, he would have been in there for only a couple days. But my sister got him out the same day! My son stayed with her for a month or two, and then he moved back to his dad's. His dad had changed. He was not the same man as he had been years ago. And for that, I am grateful!

We were all young at one point in our lives. Some of us got into trouble, and some of us didn't. I'd like to think that life's not about the trouble you get into, it's about the lesson you learn from it. What lesson are you walking away with? What have you learned from it? If you don't like the road you're on, change it. Don't make excuses, just change it. It is never to late to change the road you're on. When my sons got into trouble it hurt my soul. But they have to take responsibility for their actions and remedy the situation. Currently, they are doing everything in their power to correct any wrong doing. I love them deeply, and I am very proud of them both.

Faith in Myself

Chapter 9

Hope and Courage

A S I STATED in the beginning, this book is meant to offer hope and courage. It is meant to tell you that I care when no one else does. I am here to tell you that if family hurts you, its okay. You can go further in your life without them. I am living proof of that.

When you are down and someone kicks you and it hurts so bad in your gut, I can honestly say that I have been there. I have been kicked while I was down more times than I can possibly count. The things that I've had to endure, no one should ever have to. No one has the right to touch someone else physically or sexually. There are some people in this world who think they rule others, that they are greater than you because they can control you. But here's the kick to them. Nobody ever has the right to control someone else. If they do or they try, get away from them as soon as you can. God has a plan for everybody. He had a plan for you and me before we were even born. So no matter what you do, if you are good or bad, he will always have his plan for you. And I truly believe that.

This book is not about pointing fingers. It is about my personal experience. It is here to offer you hope and faith. If you were standing in front of me, broken, I would give you a hug. I would tell you that despite what you were told, you *are* perfect. You are a strong person. You have all the love in the world to give. I would stand you in front of your mirror and tell you that God gave you a purpose on this earth. You had to go through what you went through so that you can be strong for others.

Chapter 10

Fairness

THERE IS A ton of unfairness in the world. Every day people take advantage of the less fortunate, the little children, and the elderly. This hurts my soul so much. As much as you want and strive for a perfect world, there are so many things that need to be fixed to get it there.

I am not going to sugarcoat anything. I am not going to lie to you. If a person has wronged you, please acknowledge the fact that it wasn't your fault. You did nothing wrong. Don't blame yourself because someone else thought evil thoughts or did evil things.

Write his or her name on a piece of paper and then burn it. As it's burning say this, "I release the hold you have on me. I know that you are mentally ill. Your injustices are not going to bind my heart.

I forgive you and will let God deal with you when the time comes."

May your burdens be lifted! Feel no more guilt or pain. You are whole again. You are free. Never turn your mind back to that ever again. You have released it; you have let it go…forever.

Chapter 11

Looking Forward

YOU WILL BECOME the person you have always dreamed about. See it, visualize it, and become it. The hardest thing to try to change is the tough exterior that is always present—like you will not let anyone in your heart.

But by doing this, you are not letting *yourself* into your own heart. It is okay to feel. You have to allow yourself to feel everything. By acknowledging the pain, you are bringing awareness to it. And once you do that, you can overcome it. You have processed it. You can then move forward and accept it as it is.

Where do you want to be? Where do you want to go in your life? Who are you? What are your dreams? Are you enjoying your life? Do you have the career that you always wanted? Do you truly enjoy what it is that you are doing?

These dreams are yours. No one will ever take them away, only if you let them. Don't ever let anyone stand in your way of becoming who were meant to be! Success is yours, and you deserve it!

The hardest thing in life that you will have to overcome is fear. Fear will destroy a man fast. Its thoughts are binding and suffocating. You have to turn the fear of the unknown into a positive. Negativity and fear go hand in hand. Watch what you say and how you say it. Say only positive things and only do positive actions. By doing this you will overcome all self doubt. Don't hold on to other people's secrets, they will weight you down. They are not yours to keep. Let them go.

Despite everything that you go through in life, you have to have the ability to Walk In Peace with yourself. After you have worked through your emotions and have dealt with the fear, anger, depression, or whatever emotions you have gone through, you will be able to Walk In Peace with your life.

Find what it is you would like to do and go out and do it! There is only one you, and you only have one life. May you Walk In Peace.

2 Corinthians 1:4
Who comforts us in all our troubles, so that we can comfort those in any trouble with the comfort we ourselves have received from God.

Colossians 3:13
Bear with each other and forgive whatever grievances you may have against one another. Forgive as the Lord forgave you.

1 Peter 5:7
Cast all your anxiety on him because he cares for you.

Jeremiah 29:11
"For I know the plans I have for you," declares the Lord, "plans to prosper you and not to harm you, plans to give you a hope and a future."

John 14:27
Peace I leave with you, my peace I give you. I do not give to you as the world gives. Do not let your hearts be troubled and do not be afraid.

Psalm 9:9
The Lord is a refuge for the oppressed, a stronghold in times of trouble.

Psalm 9:10
Those who know your name will trust in you, for you, Lord, have never forsaken those who seek you.

A special thank you to Nancy Flowers for contributing some of these scriptures. Her website is http://www.TellSomebodyBooks.com

WinePressPublishing
Great Books, Defined.

To order additional copies of this book call:
1-877-421-READ (7323)
or please visit our website at
www.WinePressbooks.com

If you enjoyed this quality custom-published book,
drop by our website for more books and information.

www.winepresspublishing.com
"Your partner in custom publishing."

CPSIA information can be obtained at www.ICGtesting.com
233600LV00001B/1/P

9 781414 119700